1970

D0778511

Malcolm Mooneys' Land

by the same author

THE NIGHTFISHING
THE WHITE THRESHOLD

*

CAGE WITHOUT GRIEVANCE
(Parton Press, David Archer)

2ND POEMS
(Nicholson and Watson)

Malcolm Mooney's Land

W. S. GRAHAM

London
FABER AND FABER

First published in 1970
by Faber and Faber Limited
24 Russell Square London WC1
Reprinted 1970
Printed in Great Britain by
the Bowering Press Plymouth
All rights reserved

SBN 571 09309 4

CONTENTS

ACKNOWLEDGEMENTS

Acknowledgements are due to the
following periodicals in which some of
these poems earlier appeared:

> New Statesman
> The Listener
> The Cornish Review
> Poetry (Chicago)
> Botteghe Oscure
> The Malahat Review

The author wishes to thank The Arts
Council for a grant in the summer of 1969.

Malcolm Mooney's Land

I

Today, Tuesday, I decided to move on
Although the wind was veering. Better to move
Than have them at my heels, poor friends
I buried earlier under the printed snow.
From wherever it is I urge these words
To find their subtle vents, the northern dazzle
Of silence cranes to watch. Footprint on foot
Print, word on word and each on a fool's errand.
Malcolm Mooney's Land. Elizabeth
Was in my thoughts all morning and the boy.
Wherever I speak from or in what particular
Voice, this is always a record of me in you.
I can record at least out there to the west
The grinding bergs and, listen, further off
Where we are going, the glacier calves
Making its sudden momentary thunder.
This is as good a night, a place as any.

II

From the rimed bag of sleep, Wednesday,
My words crackle in the early air.
Thistles of ice about my chin,
My dreams, my breath a ruff of crystals.
The new ice falls from canvas walls.
O benign creature with the small ear-hole,
Submerger under silence, lead
Me where the unblubbered monster goes
Listening and makes his play.
Make my impediment mean no ill
And be itself a way.

A fox was here last night (Maybe Nansen's,
Reading my instruments.) the prints
All round the tent and not a sound.
Not that I'd have him call my name.
Anyhow how should he know? Enough
Voices are with me here and more
The further I go. Yesterday
I heard the telephone ringing deep
Down in a blue crevasse.
I did not answer it and could
Hardly bear to pass.

Landlice, always my good bedfellows,
Ride with me in my sweaty seams.
Come bonny friendly beasts, brother
To the grammarsow and the word-louse,
Bite me your presence, keep me awake
In the cold with work to do, to remember
To put down something to take back.
I have reached the edge of earshot here
And by the laws of distance
My words go through the smoking air
Changing their tune on silence.

III

My friend who loves owls
Has been with me all day
Walking at my ear
And speaking of old summers
When to speak was easy.
His eyes are almost gone
Which made him hear well.

Under our feet the great
Glacier drove its keel.
What is to read there
Scored out in the dark?

Later the north-west distance
Thickened towards us.
The blizzard grew and proved
Too filled with other voices
High and desperate
For me to hear him more.
I turned to see him go
Becoming shapeless into
The shrill swerving snow.

IV

Today, Friday, holds the white
Paper up too close to see
Me here in a white-out in this tent of a place
And why is it there has to be
Some place to find, however momentarily
To speak from, some distance to listen to?

Out at the far-off edge I hear
Colliding voices, drifted, yes
To find me through the slowly opening leads.
Tomorrow I'll try the rafted ice.
Have I not been trying to use the obstacle
Of language well? It freezes round us all.

V

Why did you choose this place
For us to meet? Sit
With me between this word
And this, my furry queen.
Yet not mistake this
For the real thing. Here
In Malcolm Mooney's Land
I have heard many
Approachers in the distance
Shouting. Early hunters
Skittering across the ice
Full of enthusiasm
And making fly and,
Within the ear, the yelling
Spear steepening to
The real prey, the right
Prey of the moment.
The honking choir in fear
Leave the tilting floe
And enter the sliding water.
Above the bergs the foolish
Voices are lighting lamps
And all their sounds make
This diary of a place
Writing us both in.

Come and sit. Or is
It right to stay here
While, outside the tent
The bearded blinded go
Calming their children
Into the ovens of frost?

And what's the news? What
Brought you here through
The spring leads opening?

Elizabeth, you and the boy
Have been with me often
Especially on those last
Stages. Tell him a story.
Tell him I came across
An old sulphur bear
Sawing his log of sleep
Loud beneath the snow.
He puffed the powdered light
Up on to this page
And here his reek fell
In splinters among
These words. He snored well.
Elizabeth, my furry
Pelted queen of Malcolm
Mooney's Land, I made
You here beside me
For a moment out
Of the correct fatigue.

I have made myself alone now.
Outside the tent endless
Drifting hummock crests.
Words drifting on words.
The real unabstract snow.

The Beast in the Space

Shut up. Shut up. There's nobody here.
If you think you hear somebody knocking
On the other side of the words, pay
No attention. It will be only
The great creature that thumps its tail
On silence on the other side.
If you do not even hear that
I'll give the beast a quick skelp
And through Art you'll hear it yelp.

The beast that lives on silence takes
Its bite out of either side.
It pads and sniffs between us. Now
It comes and laps my meaning up.
Call it over. Call it across
This curious necessary space.
Get off, you terrible inhabiter
Of silence. I'll not have it. Get
Away to whoever it is will have you.

He's gone and if he's gone to you
That's fair enough. For on this side
Of the words it's late. The heavy moth
Bangs on the pane. The whole house
Is sleeping and I remember
I am not here, only the space
I sent the terrible beast across.
Watch. He bites. Listen gently
To any song he snorts or growls
And give him food. He means neither
Well or ill towards you. Above
All, shut up. Give him your love.

The Lying Dear

At entrance cried out but not
For me (Should I have needed it?)
Her bitching eyes under
My pressing down shoulder
Looked up to meet the face
In cracks on the flaking ceiling
Descending. The map of damp
Behind me, up, formed
Itself to catch the look
Under the closed (now)
Lids of my lying dear.

Under my pinning arm
I suddenly saw between
The acting flutters, a look
Catch on some image not me.

With a hand across her eyes
I changed my weight of all
Knowledge of her before.
And like a belly sledge
I steered us on the run
Mounting the curves to almost
The high verge. Her breath
Flew out like smoke. Her beauty
Twisted into another
Beauty and we went down
Into the little village
Of a new language.

Yours Truly

In reply to your last letter
Which came in too confused
For words saying 'Listen.
And silence even has turned
Away. Listen.' Dear Pen
Pal in the distance, beyond
My means, why do you bring
Your face down so near
To affront me here again
With a new expression out
Of not indifferent eyes?
I know you well alas
From where I sit behind
The Art barrier of ice.

Did you hear me call you across
The dead centre of the night?

Where is your pride I said
To myself calling myself
By my name even pronouncing
It freshly I thought but blushed
At the lonely idea.
I saw myself wearing
A clumping taliped
Disguise I was too shy
To take an answer from.

Am I too loud? I hear
Members of the house stirring
Not able to keep asleep

Not able to keep awake
Nor to be satisfactorily
Between. O by the way
I thought I saw you standing
Older losing yourself in
The changed Mooney's mirrors
Of what is left of Ireland.

Dear Who I Mean

Dear who I mean but more
Than because of the lonely stumble
In the spiked bramble after
The wrecked dragon caught
In the five high singing wires
Its tail twisting the wind
Into visibility, I turn
To where is it you lodge
Now at the other end
Of this letter let out
On the end of its fine string
Across your silent airts.

There is more to it than just
A boy losing his kite
On a young day. My flying
Stem and cooper's hoop
And printed paper bucks
And stalls then leaves the air
I thought I had made it for.

When the word or the word's name
Flies out before us in winter
Beware of the cunning god
Slinking across the tense
Fields ready to pretend
To carry in spittled jaws
The crashed message, this letter
Between us. With two fingers
I give one whistle along
The frozen black sticks

To bring him to heel. He knows
He is better over a distance.

And now when the wind falls
Disentangle the string. Kill
The creature if so you move.
Use the material of
Its artifice. You might even
Reassemble for your own sake
A dragon to live your life with.

But the quick brown pouncing god
Magnifies towards us.
He crunches it up like a bird
And does not leave one word.

The Constructed Space

Meanwhile surely there must be something to say,
Maybe not suitable but at least happy
In a sense here between us two whoever
We are. Anyhow here we are and never
Before have we two faced each other who face
Each other now across this abstract scene
Stretching between us. This is a public place
Achieved against subjective odds and then
Mainly an obstacle to what I mean.

It is like that, remember. It is like that
Very often at the beginning till we are met
By some intention risen up out of nothing.
And even then we know what we are saying
Only when it is said and fixed and dead.
Or maybe, surely, of course we never know
What we have said, what lonely meanings are read
Into the space we make. And yet I say
This silence here for in it I might hear you.

I say this silence or, better, construct this space
So that somehow something may move across
The caught habits of language to you and me.
From where we are it is not us we see
And times are hastening yet, disguise is mortal.
The times continually disclose our home.
Here in the present tense disguise is mortal.
The trying times are hastening. Yet here I am
More truly now this abstract act become.

Master Cat and Master Me

Do Antoine Ó Máille

The way I see it is that Master
Me is falling out with Servant
Me and understairs is live
With small complaints and clattering.

The dust is being too quickly
Feathered off my dear objects.
On the other hand I find myself
Impeded where I want to go.

Even the cat (He has no name.)
Is felinely aware that Master
House's bosom is not what
It used to be. The kitchen door

Swings on its hinges singing on
A foreign pitch. The mice have new
Accents and their little scurries
Have acquired a different grace.

At this time the light is always
Anxious to go away. The mantel
Brasses flicker and Malcolm Mooney's
Walrus tooth gleams yellow.

Who let you in? Who pressed
The cracked Master's cup on you?
I will show you out through
The Master's door to the Servant world.

Dont let Master Cat out.
He has to stay and serve with me.
His Master now must enter
The service of the Master Sea.

The Thermal Stair

For the painter Peter Lanyon
killed in a gliding accident 1964

I called today, Peter, and you were away.
I look out over Botallack and over Ding
Dong and Levant and over the jasper sea.

Find me a thermal to speak and soar to you from
Over Lanyon Quoit and the circling stones standing
High on the moor over Gurnard's Head where some

Time three foxglove summers ago, you came.
The days are shortening over Little Parc Owles.
The poet or painter steers his life to maim

Himself somehow for the job. His job is Love
Imagined into words or paint to make
An object that will stand and will not move.

Peter, I called and you were away, speaking
Only through what you made and at your best.
Look, there above Botallack, the buzzard riding

The salt updraught slides off the broken air
And out of sight to quarter a new place.
The Celtic sea, the Methodist sea is there.

> You said once in the Engine
> House below Morvah
> That words make their world
> In the same way as the painter's
> Mark surprises him
> Into seeing new.

Sit here on the sparstone
In this ruin where
Once the early beam
Engine pounded and broke
The air with industry.

Now the chuck of daws
And the listening sea.

'Shall we go down' you said
'Before the light goes
And stand under the old
Tinworkings around
Morvah and St Just?'
You said 'Here is the sea
Made by alfred wallis
Or any poet or painter's
Eye it encountered.
Or is it better made
By all those vesselled men
Sometime it maintained?
We all make it again.'

Give me your hand, Peter,
To steady me on the word.

Seventy-two by sixty,
Italy hangs on the wall.
A woman stands with a drink
In some polite place
And looks at SARACINESCO
And turns to mention space.
That one if she could
Would ride Artistically
The thermals you once rode.

Peter, the phallic boys
Begin to wink their lights.
Godrevy and the Wolf
Are calling Opening Time.
We'll take the quickest way
The tin singers made.
Climb here where the hand
Will not grasp on air.
And that dark-suited man
Has set the dominoes out
On the Queen's table.
Peter, we'll sit and drink
And go in the sea's roar
To Labrador with wallis
Or rise on Lanyon's stair.

Uneasy, lovable man, give me your painting
Hand to steady me taking the word-road home.
Lanyon, why is it you're earlier away?
Remember me wherever you listen from.
Lanyon, dingdong dingdong from carn to carn.
It seems tonight all Closing bells are tolling
Across the Duchy shire wherever I turn.

I Leave This at Your Ear

(For Nessie Dunsmuir)

I leave this at your ear for when you wake,
A creature in its abstract cage asleep.
Your dreams blindfold you by the light they make.

The owl called from the naked-woman tree
As I came down by the Kyle farm to hear
Your house silent by the speaking sea.

I have come late but I have come before
Later with slaked steps from stone to stone
To hope to find you listening for the door.

I stand in the ticking room. My dear, I take
A moth kiss from your breath. The shore gulls cry.
I leave this at your ear for when you wake.

The Dark Dialogues

I

I always meant to only
Language swings away
Further before me.

Language swings away
Before me as I go
With again the night rising
Up to accompany me
And that other fond
Metaphor, the sea.
Images of night
And the sea changing
Should know me well enough.

Wanton with riding lights
And staring eyes, Europa
And her high meadow bull
Fall slowly their way
Behind the blindfold and
Across this more or less
Uncommon place.

And who are you and by
What right do I waylay
You where you go there
Happy enough striking
Your hobnail in the dark?
Believe me I would ask
Forgiveness but who
Would I ask forgiveness from?

I speak across the vast
Dialogues in which we go
To clench my words against
Time or the lack of time
Hoping that for a moment
They will become for me
A place I can think in
And think anything in,
An aside from the monstrous.

And this is no other
Place than where I am,
Here turning between
This word and the next.
Yet somewhere the stones
Are wagging in the dark
And you, whoever you are,
That I am other to,
Stand still by the glint
Of the dyke's sparstone,
Because always language
Is where the people are.

II

Almost I, yes, I hear
Huge in the small hours
A man's step on the stair
Climbing the pipeclayed flights
And then stop still
Under the stairhead gas
At the lonely tenement top.
The broken mantle roars
Or dims to a green murmur.

One door faces another.
Here, this is the door
With the loud grain and the name
Unreadable in brass.
Knock, but a small knock,
The children are asleep.
I sit here at the fire
And the children are there
And in this poem I am,
Whoever elsewhere I am,
Their mother through his mother.
I sit with the gas turned
Down and time knocking
Somewhere through the wall.
Wheesht, children, and sleep
As I break the raker up,
It is only the stranger
Hissing in the grate.
Only to speak and say
Something, little enough,
Not out of want
Nor out of love, to say
Something and to hear
That someone has heard me.
This is the house I married
Into, a room and kitchen
In a grey tenement,
The top flat of the land,
And I hear them breathe and turn
Over in their sleep
As I sit here becoming
Hardly who I know.
I have seen them hide
And seek and cry come out

Come out whoever you are
You're not het I called
And called across the wide
Wapenschaw of water.
But the place moved away
Beyond the reach of any
Word. Only the dark
Dialogues drew their breath.
Ah how bright the mantel
Brass shines over me.
Black-lead at my elbow,
Pipe-clay at my feet.
Wheesht and go to sleep
And grow up but not
To say mother mother
Where are the great games
I grew up quick to play.

III

Now in the third voice
I am their father through
Nothing more than where
I am made by this word
And this word to occur.
Here I am makeshift made
By artifice to fall
Upon a makeshift time.
But I can't see. I can't
See in the bad light
Moving (Is it moving?)
Between your eye and mine.
Who are you and yet
It doesn't matter only

I thought I heard somewhere
Someone else walking.
Where are the others? Why,
If there is any other,
Have they gone so far ahead?
Here where I am held
With the old rainy oak
And Cartsburn and the Otter's
Burn aroar in the dark
I try to pay for my keep.
I speak as well as I can
Trying to teach my ears
To learn to use their eyes
Even only maybe
In the end to observe
The behaviour of silence.
Who is it and why
Do you walk here so late
And how should you know to take
The left or the right fork
Or the way where, as a boy
I used to lie crouched
Deep under the flailing
Boughs of the roaring wood?
Or I lay still
Listening while a branch
Squeaked in the resinous dark
And swaying silences.

Otherwise I go
Only as a shell
Of my former self.
I go with my foot feeling
To find the side of the road,

My head inclined, my ears
Feathered to every wind
Blown between the dykes.
The mist is coming home.
I hear the blind horn
Mourning from the firth.
The big wind blows
Over the shore of my child
Hood in the off-season.
The small wind remurmurs
The fathering tenement
And a boy I knew running
The hide and seeking streets.
Or do these winds
In their forces blow
Between the words only?

I am the shell held
To Time's ear and you
May hear the lonely leagues
Of the kittiwake and the fulmar.

IV

Or I am always only
Thinking is this the time
To look elsewhere to turn
Towards what was it
I put myself out
Away from home to meet?
Was it this only? Surely
It is more than these words
See on my side
I went halfway to meet.

And there are other times.
But the times are always
Other and now what I meant
To say or hear or be
Lies hidden where exile
Too easily beckons.
What if the terrible times
Moving away find
Me in the end only
Staying where I am always
Unheard by a fault.

So to begin to return
At last neither early
Nor late and go my way
Somehow home across
This gesture become
Inhabited out of hand.
I stop and listen over
My shoulder and listen back
On language for that step
That seems to fall after
My own step in the dark.

Always must be the lost
Or where we turn, and all
For a sight of the dark again.
The farthest away, the least
To answer back come nearest.

And this place is taking
Its time from us though these
Two people or voices
Are not us nor has

The time they seem to move in
To do with what we think
Our own times are. Even
Where they are is only
This one inhuman place.
Yet somewhere a stone
Speaks and maybe a leaf
In the dark turns over.
And whoever I meant
To think I had met
Turns away further
Before me blinded by
This word and this word.

See how presently
The bull and the girl turn
From what they seemed to say,
And turn there above me
With that star-plotted head
Snorting on silence.
The legend turns. And on
Her starry face descried
Faintly astonishment.
The formal meadow fades
Over the ever-widening
Firth and in their time
That not unnatural pair
Turn slowly home.

This is no other place
Than where I am, between
This word and the next.
Maybe I should expect
To find myself only

Saying that again
Here now at the end.
Yet over the great
Gantries and cantilevers
Of love, a sky, real and
Particular is slowly
Startled into light.

The Don Brown Route

Over your head the climbing blue
Sky observes your lonely foot.
Through the lens of language I
Focus on the Don Brown Route.

From where I am, even if I shout,
You will not hear. You climb in slow
Motion on silence on the face
Full of happy, full of woe.

Today is very nothing like
Any other day that once soared
In this place. My lens suddenly
Is crossed with the black of a near bird.

Today is almost without winds
And I can see your fingers brush
Your next hold clean and the sand drift
Fine like the smoke of your own ash.

Through the lens of language each
Act hangs for a long time.
Floated out in the iodine air
Your motion comes to me like home

Ing birds meaning to say something
I should be able to read. Reach
For the hold three feet above your pressing
Cheek bright at the edge of your stretch.

Set your Northern toe-cap in
To where your own weather has set
A ledge of spar like an offered journey
Across the cobbles of your street.

At least I am not putting you off
Through the dumb lens I see you through.
I can't nudge your climbing foot
Or shout out to you what to do.

Yet do not lean too far in
To the father face or it will
Astonish you with a granite kiss
And send you packing over the sill.

If you fall, remember no one will see
You tumbling lonely down. Only
I through this bad focus will see.
Why do you imagine Gravity lonely?

And over your head the climbing blue
Sky observes your lonely foot.
Stopped in the lens of language you
Slowly establish the Don Brown Route.

Press Button to Hold Desired Symbol

King William the Fourth's electric One
Armed Bandit rolls its eyes to Heaven.
Churchtown Madron's Garfield Strick
Stands at the moment less than even

Garfield, pull down the mystic arm
And let the holy cylinders turn.
His wife is stirring jam at home
In a copper pan with damsons in.

Plums, oranges and yellow bells
Bite at the worship of his eye.
A small dog stirs at his feet
Making a woolly soundless cry.

O try again, Garfield Strick.
The electric fruit can drop or fly.
The paradisical orchard goes
Upward with a clicking cry.

Untouched by nature spins the fruit
Of an orchard of magic seed.
Do not disturb. The oracle rolls
Its eyes too fast for him to read.

And stops. King William the Fourth pays out
With a line of clattering oranges.
Garfield turns. His glass shatters
Its shape in our astonished gaze.

In the high air on thin sticks
The blanched rags in the wind blow.
The brass cylinder turns round
Saying I know I know I know.

Hilton Abstract

Roger, whether the tree is made
To speak or stand as a tree should
Lifting its branches over lovers
And moving as the wind moves,
It is the longed-for, loved event,
To be by another aloneness loved.

Hell with this and hell with that
And hell with all the scunnering lot.
This can go and that can go
And leave us with the quick and slow.
And quick and slow are nothing much.
We either touch or do not touch.

Yet the great humilities
Keep us always ill at ease.
The weather moves above us and
The mouse makes its little sound.
Whatever happens happens and
The false hands are moving round.

Hell with this and hell with that.
All that's best is better not.
Yet the great humilities
Keep us always ill at ease,
And in keeping us they go
Through the quick and through the slow.

Approaches to How They Behave

I

What does it matter if the words
I choose, in the order I choose them in,
Go out into a silence I know
Nothing about, there to be let
In and entertained and charmed
Out of their master's orders? And yet
I would like to see where they go
And how without me they behave.

II

Speaking is difficult and one tries
To be exact and yet not to
Exact the prime intention to death.
On the other hand the appearance of things
Must not be made to mean another
Thing. It is a kind of triumph
To see them and to put them down
As what they are. The inadequacy
Of the living, animal language drives
Us all to metaphor and an attempt
To organize the spaces we think
We have made occur between the words.

III

The bad word and the bad word and
The word which glamours me with some
Quick face it pulls to make me let
It leave me to go across

In roughly your direction, hates
To go out maybe so completely
On another silence not its own.

IV

Before I know it they are out
Afloat in the head which freezes them.
Then I suppose I take the best
Away and leave the others arranged
Like floating bergs to sink a convoy.

V

One word says to its mate O
I do not think we go together
Are we doing any good here
Why do we find ourselves put down?
The mate pleased to be spoken to
Looks up from the line below
And says well that doubtful god
Who has us here is far from sure
How we on our own tickle the chin
Of the prince or the dame that lets us in.

VI

The dark companion is a star
Very present like a dark poem
Far and unreadable just out
At the edge of this poem floating.
It is not more or less a dark
Companion poem to the poem.

VII

Language is expensive if
We want to strut, busked out
Showing our best on silence.
Good Morning. That is a bonny doing
Of verbs you wear with the celandine
Catching the same sun as mine.
You wear your dress like a prince but
A country's prince beyond my ken.
Through the chinks in your lyric coat
My ear catches a royal glimpse
Of fuzzed flesh, unworded body.
Was there something you wanted to say?
I myself dress up in what I can
Afford on the broadway. Underneath
My overcoat of the time's slang
I am fashionable enough wearing
The grave-clothes of my generous masters.

VIII

And what are you supposed to say
I asked a new word but it kept mum.
I had secretly admired always
What I thought it was here for.
But I was wrong when I looked it up
Between the painted boards. It said
Something it was never very likely
I could fit in to a poem in my life.

IX

The good word said I am not pressed
For time. I have all the foxglove day

And all my user's days to give
You my attention. Shines the red
Fox in the digitalis grove.
Choose me choose me. Guess which
Word I am here calling myself
The best. If you can't fit me in
To lying down here among the fox
Glove towers of the moment, say
I am yours the more you use me. Tomorrow
Same place same time give me a ring.

X

Backwards the poem's just as good.
We human angels as we read
Read back as we gobble the words up.
Allowing the poem to represent
A recognizable landscape
Sprouting green up or letting green
With all its weight of love hang
To gravity's sweet affection,
Arse-versa it is the same object,
Even although the last word seems
To have sung first, or the breakfast lark
Sings up from the bottom of the sea.

XI

The poem is not a string of knots
Tied for a meaning of another time
And country, unreadable, found
By chance. The poem is not a henge
Or Easter Island emerged Longnose
Or a tally used by early unknown

Peoples. The words we breathe and puff
Are our utensils down the dream
Into the manhole. Replace the cover.

XII

The words are mine. The thoughts are all
Yours as they occur behind
The bat of your vast unseen eyes.
These words are as you see them put
Down on the dead-still page. They have
No ability above their station.
Their station on silence is exact.
What you do with them is nobody's business.

XIII

Running across the language lightly
This morning in the hangingover
Whistling light from the window, I
Was tripped and caught into the whole
Formal scheme which Art is.
I had only meant to enjoy
Dallying between the imaginary
And imaginary's opposite
With a thought or two up my sleeve.

XIV

Is the word? Yes Yes. But I hear
A sound without words from another
Person I can't see at my elbow.
A sigh to be proud of. You? Me?

XV

Having to construct the silence first
To speak out on I realize
The silence even itself floats
At my ear-side with a character
I have not met before. Hello
Hello I shout but that silence
Floats steady, will not be marked
By an off-hand shout. For some reason
It refuses to be broken now
By what I thought was worth saying.
If I wait a while, if I look out
At the heavy greedy rooks on the wall
It will disperse. Now I construct
A new silence I hope to break.

The Fifteen Devices

When who we think we are is suddenly
Flying apart, splintered into
Acts we hardly recognize
As once our kin's curious children,
I find myself turning my head
Round to observe and strangely
Accept expected astonishments
Of myself manifest and yet
Bereft somehow as I float
Out in an old-fashioned slow
Motion in all directions. I hope
A value is there lurking somewhere.

Whether it is the words we try
To hold on to or some other
Suggestion of outsideness at least
Not ourselves, it is a naked
State extremely uncomfortable.

My fifteen devices of shadow and brightness
Are settling in and the Madron
Morning accepts them in their places.
Early early the real as any
Badger in the black wood
Of Madron is somewhere going
His last round, a creature of words
Waiting to be asked to help me
In my impure, too-human purpose.

With me take you. Where shall you find us?
Somewhere here between the prised

Open spaces between the flying
Apart words. For then it was
All the blown, black wobblers
Came over on the first wind
To let me see themselves looking
In from a better high flocking
Organization than mine. They make
Between them a flag flying standing
For their own country. Down the Fore
Street run the young to the school bell.

Shall I pull myself together into
Another place? I can't follow
The little young clusters of thoughts
Running down the summer side.

My fifteen devices in my work
Shop of shadow and brightness have
Their places as they stand ready
To go out to say Hello.

Wynter and the Grammarsow

SOUND a long blast
Of silence CUT

Sir Longlegged Liker you
Of the Royal Grammarsow
Under its great slate,
I bow in my disguise
And give you your titles.

SOUND the water organ
Of the Greek CUT

Bryan the Spinner
In endless eddies
Above the weir
Of rushing home.

Fibre-glass swiveller
Over the weaving
Strands of water
In an innocent pool.

Scholar King
Of rare meanders.
Rider of Rivers
Undiscovered.

Nightwalker beside the dykes
Blown like mouthorgans
By the Atlantic wind.

Walker beside the star
Lit fences of Housman.
Black-rod of Ernst's
Beaked politicians.

Masked thinskinned diver
On the Cornish shelf.
Wet-suited Seeker after
The church choir of urchins.

SOUND Beddoes towards us
Saying singing I see
His life as on a map of rivers CUT

II

Bryan the Couth.
Brave of the Sue.
King of the Whirr
Of the windmill.
Perambulator
Of the Christian Fields.
Charming Monotype.
Failed Prefect.
King of the Blue
Pebbled Peepers.
King of Mon.
Truant to Age.

III

SOUND a Wyntermade
Disturbance of what
We expect light to do.
Hold it Hold it CUT

King the Uncrude. King Aggravator
Of Monkeys. Campion of the Gram
Marsow painting blindly under
Its timeless tons of granite thunder.

Long upperlipped king of the dark vowels.
Charmer of brash northern beasts.
Enthusiast King in the making
Of what your subjects have never seen.

Momaster, Ravenmaster, Caneless
Housemaster of a good family.
Master Ventriloquist of fashioned
Spiders. Doubtful Ringmaster of
The successful circus of your despairs.

IV

SOUND MacBryde's Song
And thus spak Willie Peden
As he sat beneath the tree
O will you wear a forgivemenot
And plant a yew for me. CUT

Confronted with what you do I can never
Find anything (not unnaturally)
To say. Of course I try to separate
Any regard for you from the made
Object before me. Maybe in a kind
Of way it is legitimate to let
One's self be added to, to be moved
By both at once, by the idea
Of the person, and the object
Adrift stationary in its Art law.

Anyhow I think you must be pretty
Good by the way I think you behave.

SOUND Yours Truly saying with an invisible voice
From the Clydeside welding cradles and the hammering
Nightshift town of Greenock, let's to grips.
Is a chat with me your fancy? Now in the dark
Give me the password. Wince me your grip for O
The times are calling us in and the little babes
Are shouldering arms in the cause of the Future Past.
Are we too old to walk around in the round?
Or have our foxes' throats been bitten through?
I dont really mean to speak to you intimately.
Finish here of Yours Truly. Please please CUT.

            The titles are finished
            It was a way
            Of speaking towards you.

     Maybe we could have a word before I go,
     As I usually say. I mean there must be some
     Way to speak together straighter than this,
     As I usually say. There is not a long time
     To go between the banks of rubbish and nature
     Down to the old beginning of the real sea.

            SOUND Coda of one Raven
            Being a black ghost
            Over the Carn CUT

     And that is why I think you think kindly
     Of the Grammarsow under its great slate.
     The W of Wynter is blown is wisped is faltered
     Off to the rivers. Applicable titles are endless.

I leave you now retreating backwards from
The cocked ear of Wynter the King standing
Good-mannered up to let me go and turn
Round in the other direction. I leave the Royal
Grammarsow King under his great slate.

Johann Joachim Quantz's First Lesson

So that each person may quickly find that
Which particularly concerns him, certain metaphors
Convenient to us within the compass of this
Lesson are to be allowed. It is best I sit
Here where I am to speak on the other side
Of language. You, of course, in your own time
And incident (I speak in the small hours.)
Will listen from your side. I am very pleased
We have sought us out. No doubt you have read
My Flute Book. Come. The Guild clock's iron men
Are striking out their few deserted hours
And here from my high window Brueghel's winter
Locks the canal below. I blow my fingers.

Five Visitors to Madron

I

In the small hours on the other side
Of language with my chair drawn
Up to the frightening abstract
Table of silence, taps. A face
Of white feathers turns my head
To suddenly see between the mad
Night astragals her looking in
Or wanted this to happen. She
Monster muse old bag or. Something
Dreamed is yes you're welcome always
Desired to drop in. It was your bleached
Finger on the pane which startled me
Although I half-expected you
But not you as you are but whoever
Would have looked in instead, another
More to my liking, not so true.

He realized it was a mistake. Closing
The door of the tomb afterwards
Secretly he thanked whoever
He could imagine to thank, some quick
Thought up thankable god of the moment.

II

As slow as distant spray falling
On the nether rocks of a headland never
Encountered but through the eye, the first
Of morning's ghost in blue palely
Hoisted my reluctant lid.

Watch what you say I said and watched
The day I uttered taking shape
To hide me in its bright bosom.

Like struck flints black flocking jack
Daws wheel over the Madron roofs.

III

I am longing not really longing
For what dont tell me let me think.
Or else I have to settle for
That step is that a step outside
At my back a new eddy of air?

And left these words at a loss to know
What form stood watching behind me
Reading us over my shoulder. I said
Now that you have come to stand
There rank-breathed at my elbow I will
Not be put off. This message must
Reach the others without your help.

IV

And met the growing gaze willing
To give its time to me to let
Itself exchange discernments
If that surely it said is what
I wanted. Quick panics put out
A field of images round me to
Look back out at it from and not
Be gazed out of all composure.
And found my research ridiculously

Ending forced to wear a mask
Of a held-up colander to peer
Through as the even gaze began
Slowly to abate never having asked
Me if I had recognized an old
Aspect of need there once my own.

Terror-spots itch on my face now.
My mind is busy hanging up
Back in their places imagination's
Clever utensils. I scratch my cheek.

V

When the fifth came I had barely drawn
A breath in to identify who
I newly am in my new old house
In Madron near the slaughterhouse.

The hint was as though a child running
Late for school cried and seemed
To have called my name in the morning
Hurrying and my name's wisp
Elongated. Leaves me here
Nameless at least very without
That name mine ever to be called
In that way different again.

Clusters Travelling Out

I

Clearly I tap to you clearly
Along the plumbing of the world
I do not know enough, not
Knowing where it ends. I tap
And tap to interrupt silence into
Manmade durations making for this
Moment a dialect for our purpose.
TAPTAP. Are you reading that taptap
I send out to you along
My element? O watch. Here they come
Opening and shutting Communication's
Gates as they approach, History's
Princes with canisters of gas
Crystals to tip and snuff me out
Strangled and knotted with my kind
Under the terrible benevolent roof.

Clearly they try to frighten me
To almost death. I am presuming
You know who I am. To answer please
Tap tap quickly along the nearest
Metal. When you hear from me
Again I will not know you. Whoever
Speaks to you will not be me.
I wonder what I will say.

II

Remember I am here O not else
Where in this quick disguise, this very

Thought that's yours for a moment. I sit
Here behind this tempered mesh.

I think I hear you hearing me.
I think I see you seeing me.
I suppose I am really only about
Two feet away. You must excuse
Me, have I spoken to you before?
I seem to know your face from some
One else I was, that particular
Shadow head on the other side
Of the wire in the VISITORS ROOM

I am learning to speak here in a way
Which may be useful afterwards.
Slops in hand we shuffle together,
Something to look forward to
Behind the spyhole. Here in our concrete
Soundbox we slide the jargon across
The watching air, a lipless language
Necessarily squashed from the side
To make its point against the rules.
It is our poetry such as it is.

Are you receiving those clusters
I send out travelling? Alas
I have no way of knowing or
If I am overheard here.
Is that (It is.) not what I want?

The slaughterhouse is next door.
Destroy this. They are very strict.

III

Can you see my As and Ys semaphore
Against the afterglow on the slaughterhouse
Roof where I stand on the black ridge
Waving my flagging arms to speak?

IV

Corridors have their character. I know well
The ring of government boots on our concrete.
Malcolm's gone now. There's nobody to shout to.
But when they're not about in the morning I shout
HOY HOY HOY and the whole corridor rings
And I listen while my last HOY turns the elbow
With a fading surprised difference of tone and loses
Heart and in dwindling echoes vanishes away.
Each person who comes, their purpose precedes them
In how they walk. You learn to read that.
Sometimes the step's accompanied by metal
Jingling and metrical, filled with invention.
Metal opened and slammed is frightening. I try
To not be the first to speak. There is nothing to say.
Burn this. I do not dislike this place. I like
Being here. They are very kind. It's doing me good.

V

If this place I write from is real then
I must be allegorical. Or maybe
The place and myself are both the one
Side of the allegory and the other
Side is apart and still escaped

Outside. And where do you come in
With your musical key-ring and brilliant
Whistle pitched for the whipped dog?

And stands loving to recover me,
Lobe-skewers clipped to his swelling breast,
His humane-killer draped with a badged
Towel white as snow. And listen,
Ventriloquized for love his words
Gainsay any deep anguish left
For the human animal. O dear night
Cover up my beastly head.

VI

Take note of who stands at my elbow listening
To all I say but not to all you hear.
She comes on Wednesdays, just on Wednesdays,
And today I make a Wednesday. On and off
I decide to make her my half-cousin Brigit
Back from the wrack and shingle on the Long Loch.
You yourself need pretend nothing. She
Is only here as an agent. She could not
On her own carry a message to you either
Written or dreamed by word of her perfect mouth.

Look. Because my words are stern and frown
She is somewhere wounded. She goes away. You see
It hasn't been a good Wednesday for her. For you
Has it been a good Wednesday? Or is yours Tuesday?

VII

When the birds blow like burnt paper
Over the poorhouse roof and the slaughter
House and all the houses of Madron,
I would like to be out of myself and
About the extra, ordinary world
No matter what disguise it wears
For my sake, in my love.

It would be better than beside the Dnieper,
The Brahmaputra or a green daughter
Tributary of the Amazon.

But first I must empty my shit-bucket
And hope my case (if it can be found)
Will come up soon. I thought I heard
My name whispered on the vine.

Surrounded by howls the double-shifting
Slaughterhouse walls me in. High
On the wall I have my blue square
Through which I see the London-Cairo
Route floating like distant feathers.

I hear their freezing whistles. Reply
Carefully. They are cracking down.
Don't hurry away. I am waiting for
A message to come in now.